STEPHEN

The COURAGEOUS Series
BOOK 1

GOD'S COURAGEOUS WITNESS

VOMBOOKS
The Voice of the Martyrs

Stephen: God's Courageous Witness

VOM Books
1815 SE Bison Rd.
Bartlesville, OK 74006

ISBN 978-0-88264-207-9

Written by The Voice of the Martyrs with Cheryl Odden

Illustrated by G. R. Erlan

Printed in China

CPC-201908p001f2

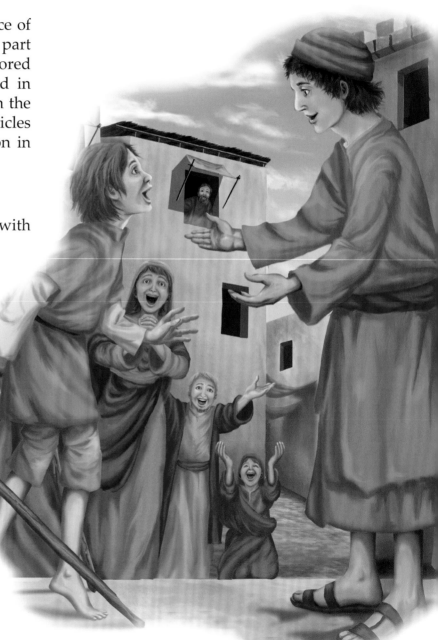

For those who boldly witness for Christ

A Note to Parents and Educators

E ven before His ascension to heaven, Jesus told the apostles, "But you will receive power when the Holy Spirit has come upon you, and you will be my witnesses in Jerusalem and in all Judea and Samaria, and to the ends of the earth" (Acts 1:8). Being a witness, or translated into the Greek "martyr," was a condition for following Jesus.

After Jesus ascended, the apostles were ridiculed by Jewish leaders who were determined to stamp out their "heretical" claims about Jesus being the Son of God, His virgin birth, and His resurrection. And Jewish scholars certainly did not want this new religion, later known as Christianity, to spread beyond Jerusalem's walls. So they set out to destroy the early church. (Decades later the Romans would become the primary persecutors of the early church.)

Jewish leaders, in an attempt to quell the popularity of the gospel of Christ, conspired against the apostles. The apostles were arrested, flogged, imprisoned, and ordered not to speak of Jesus. But they continued to speak courageously about Christ. The Sadducees threatened to kill all the apostles. But a Pharisee, Gamaliel, stopped them. He had seen this type of "heresy" before and he insisted that it would blow over. "Men of Israel," he told the Sadducees, "take care what you are about to do with these men.... for if this plan or this undertaking is of man, it will fail; but if it is of God, you will not be able to overthrow them. You might even be found opposing God!" (Acts 5:35–39). Gamaliel's words proved prophetic.

It is amid this deep hostility toward the young church that Christianity saw its first martyr, and it was not one of the apostles, but a man named Stephen.

More is known about Stephen's death than his life. Some believe that Stephen, like many disciples of the early church, was born a Jew. Many believe he was a Hellenistic (Greek-speaking) Jew because in his eloquence he could easily relate to these new converts to Christ. When some Hellenistic Jews, who were now Christ's followers, complained to the apostles about the widows in their community not getting enough to eat, the apostles appointed Stephen to assist them. Stephen was "a man full of faith and the Holy Spirit," and the apostles chose him and six others to care for the widows.

A gifted speaker with a passion for the gospel, Stephen was one of the early church's first apologists, a defender of the faith through debate. The Bible says he also performed miracles before the people.

Incensed by his speech, the Libertines or Freedmen, a group of Jews from Cyrene and Alexandria, set out to debate Stephen about Christ. But the Bible says they could not "resist the wisdom and the Spirit by which he spoke." When they could not outwit him, they tried to spread deception. They convinced others to spread lies about Stephen, assuring other Jewish leaders that he spoke against Moses and God. It was not long before Stephen was dragged into a Jewish court overseen by the Sanhedrin.

The rest is widely known and is illustrated throughout this book. What makes Stephen's life worth studying, though, is not just the circumstances of his death, but the blessing of God that flowed because of it.

Stephen's life and his subsequent death for the faith embody the importance and inspirational legacy of today's persecuted church. For in Stephen's martyrdom we see the beginning of the spread of Christianity, brought on by persecution and fueled by the courage of Christ's followers.

The Bible says even on the very day of Stephen's death "a great persecution arose against the church which was at Jerusalem." Christians were scattered throughout Judea and Samaria. And they preached the gospel everywhere they went.

After Stephen's death the early church grew greatly. In addition, one of the Jews who witnessed Stephen's arrest and stoning, Saul, became Paul, the most prolific Christian evangelist who ever lived.

May your children be inspired by the courage and boldness of Stephen's faith!

When Jesus returned to heaven, He left behind His followers. But they were not alone or without help.

As promised, Jesus sent His Holy Spirit. He knew the Holy Spirit would give His followers the strength and courage they needed to do His work.

One of these followers was Stephen.

With the Holy Spirit's help, Stephen courageously told others about Jesus and performed miracles.

He was so good at convincing others to follow Jesus that in the end Jewish leaders tried to stop him.

But first, Stephen was given an important job.

9

A man stood before the twelve apostles who walked with Jesus. "Our widows are not receiving the food they need," he said.

The apostles listened to him and nodded in agreement. They spent so much time praying and teaching about Jesus that they could not do all the work. So they decided to select seven men who were full of faith and the Holy Spirit. One of these men was Stephen.

12

Stephen and the other six men helped the widows, while the apostles preached at the Temple where the Jews worshiped.

More people chose to follow Jesus, and the church grew.

13

Stephen also loved telling people about Jesus.

And like the apostles, he healed people and performed miracles in the name of Jesus. Many were amazed with Stephen's words and actions, and turned away from their religion to follow Christ.

14

16

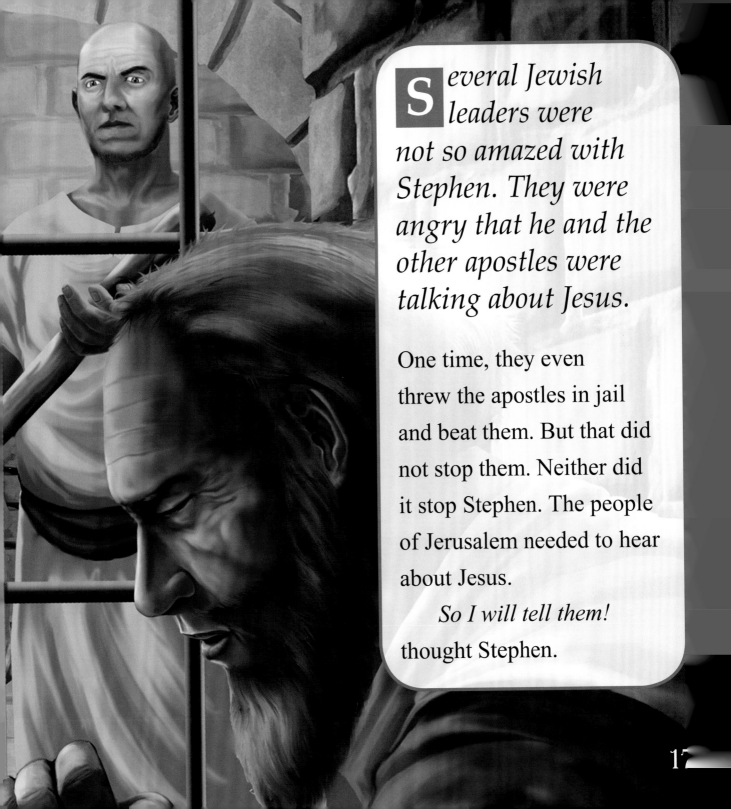

Several Jewish leaders were not so amazed with Stephen. They were angry that he and the other apostles were talking about Jesus.

One time, they even threw the apostles in jail and beat them. But that did not stop them. Neither did it stop Stephen. The people of Jerusalem needed to hear about Jesus.

So I will tell them! thought Stephen.

One day, Stephen stood before a crowd at the market. People wanted to hear what he had to say. But before Stephen could speak, a group of religious men pushed the people aside and marched up to him.

"Why are you telling others about God out here and not in our synagogue or the Temple?" asked one.

"We can talk about God anywhere," replied Stephen, "not just in a building."

The men argued with Stephen, but they were no match for him. He had an answer for every question.

"We must stop him," whispered one of the men. "The people are taking sides with him."

"How do we do that? Our men cannot compete with his wisdom."

"Leave that up to me," said another who had joined the growing crowd at the market. He smoothed out his robe and glared at Stephen, then sneaked away to carry out his plan.

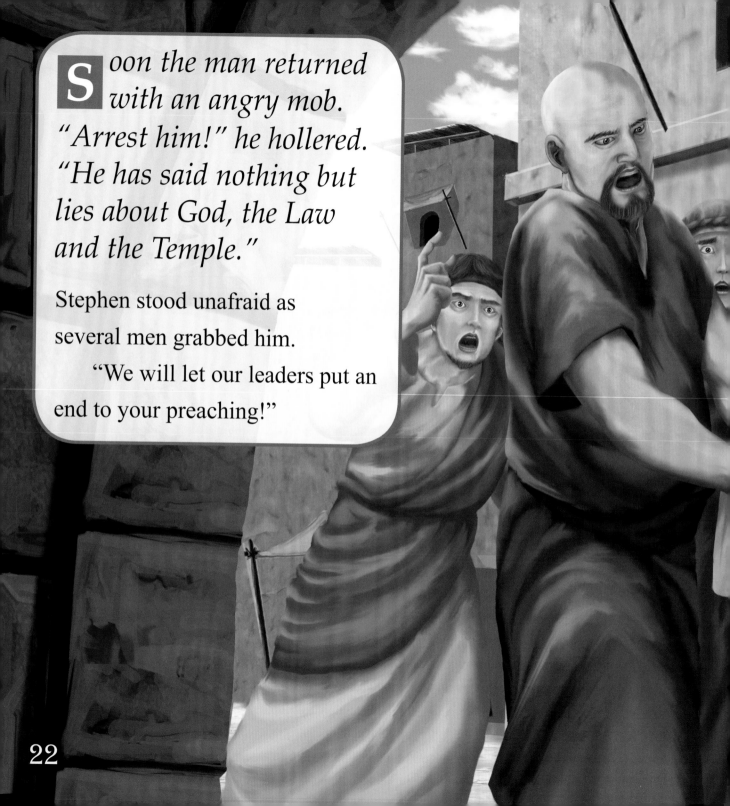

Soon the man returned with an angry mob. "Arrest him!" he hollered. "He has said nothing but lies about God, the Law and the Temple."

Stephen stood unafraid as several men grabbed him.

"We will let our leaders put an end to your preaching!"

24

A cloud of dust and a growing crowd followed Stephen and the group of Jewish leaders. Those Stephen passed sneered at him.

"How could he say such things about God?" they murmured.

Word of his arrest quickly spread throughout the city.

25

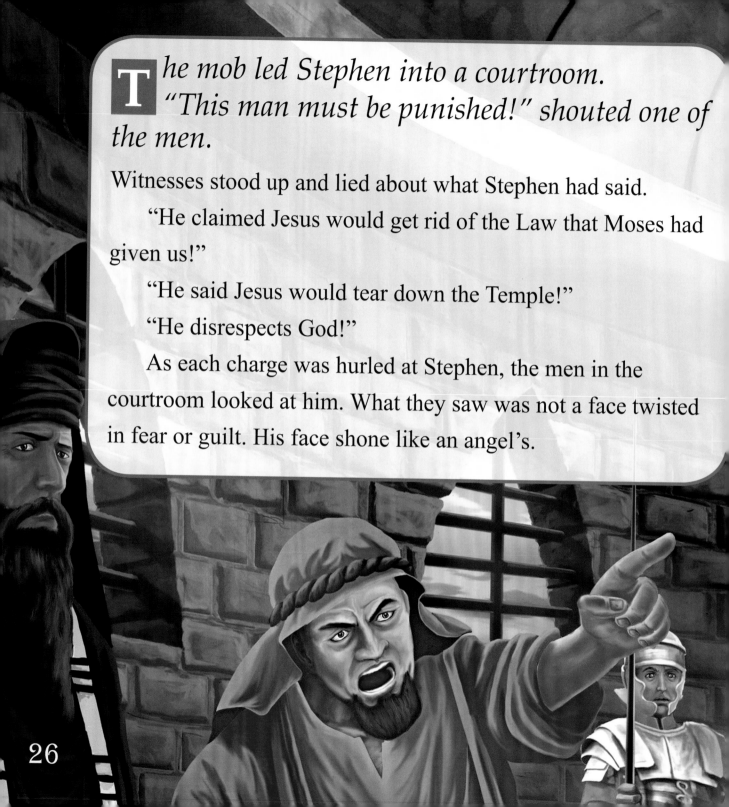

The mob led Stephen into a courtroom. *"This man must be punished!"* shouted one of the men.

Witnesses stood up and lied about what Stephen had said.

"He claimed Jesus would get rid of the Law that Moses had given us!"

"He said Jesus would tear down the Temple!"

"He disrespects God!"

As each charge was hurled at Stephen, the men in the courtroom looked at him. What they saw was not a face twisted in fear or guilt. His face shone like an angel's.

T*he chief religious leader stood up to get a better look at Stephen.*

"Is this true?" he asked. "Are you saying such things?"

"God gave Moses the Law and made him your leader," replied Stephen as he courageously looked into the crowd. He then talked about David and Solomon, who had loved the Temple.

The people crammed closer together to listen to Stephen. Not one word disrespected God, the Law, or the Temple. At first the religious leaders thought these charges were nothing but a misunderstanding. But Stephen's final words changed their minds.

S tephen took a breath. "Jesus was God's chosen one, yet your fathers persecuted those who said He was coming," he declared. "Then you killed Him!"

Stephen knew these words would anger the men in the courtroom. Still, he wanted them to know the truth about Jesus. He wanted them to have the eternal life that Christ promises.

"Enough!" shouted the chief leader over the roar of the crowd.

The people were so furious that they clenched their teeth. But Stephen did not look at them. He looked up and could not believe what he saw.

"I see heaven opened up," he announced, "and Jesus standing at God's right hand!"

31

The men dragged Stephen from the courtroom into the streets.

They threw him on the ground and began pelting him with rocks. They had made up their minds. Like Jesus, Stephen had to die.

A Jewish man named Saul watched as the leaders hit Stephen over and over again.

S tephen's feet slipped on the dry earth as the rocks hit his body.

"Kill him!" the mob cried. "Silence him for good!"

But Stephen was not angry or afraid. Instead, he prayed, "Jesus, take my spirit."

Once again, Stephen fell to his knees. "Lord, don't hold this sin against them!" he shouted over the howling mob. He hoped they could hear that he had forgiven them.

One more stone hit Stephen, and he fell to the ground and died.

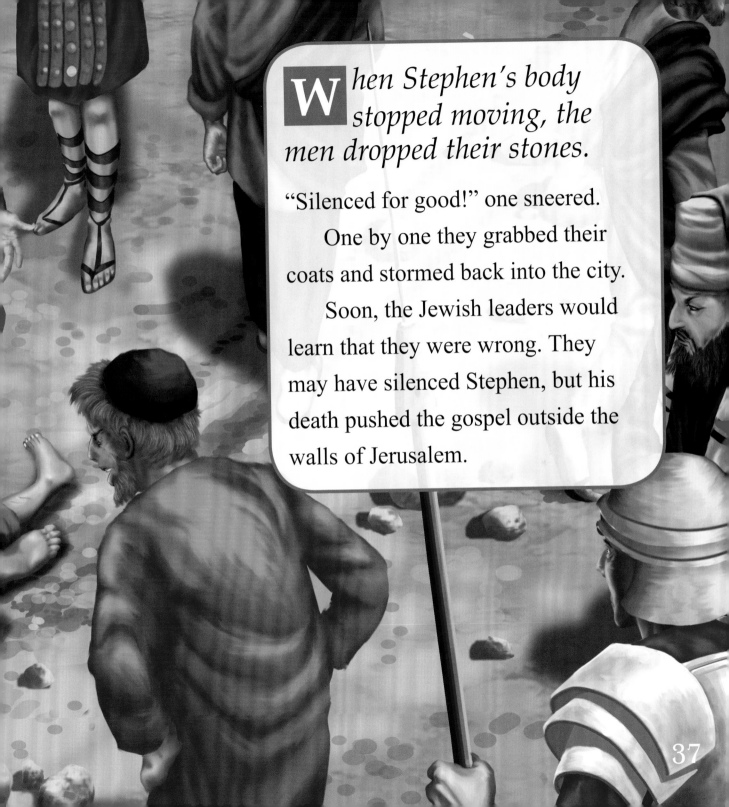

When Stephen's body stopped moving, the men dropped their stones.

"Silenced for good!" one sneered.

One by one they grabbed their coats and stormed back into the city.

Soon, the Jewish leaders would learn that they were wrong. They may have silenced Stephen, but his death pushed the gospel outside the walls of Jerusalem.

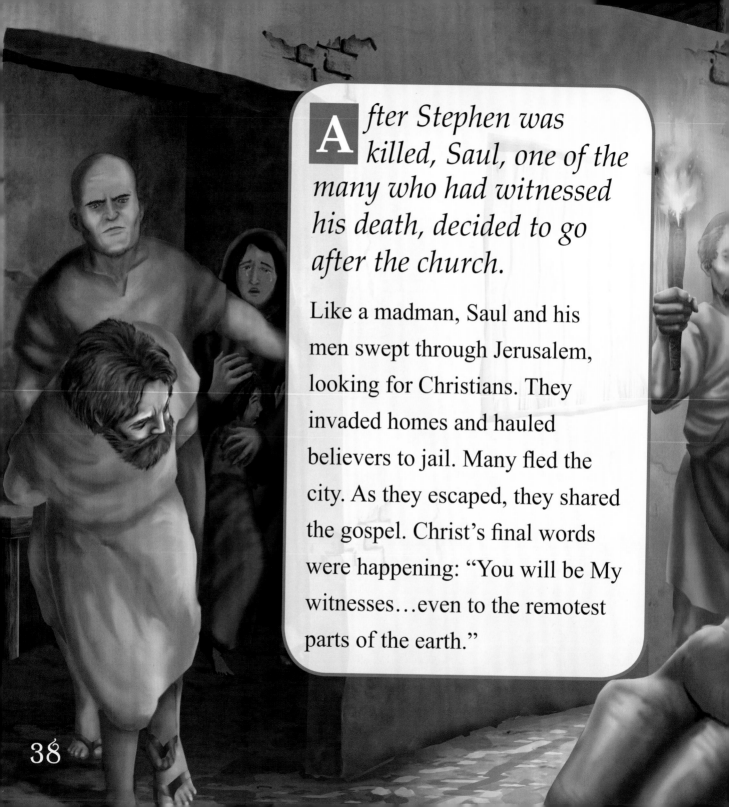

After Stephen was killed, Saul, one of the many who had witnessed his death, decided to go after the church.

Like a madman, Saul and his men swept through Jerusalem, looking for Christians. They invaded homes and hauled believers to jail. Many fled the city. As they escaped, they shared the gospel. Christ's final words were happening: "You will be My witnesses…even to the remotest parts of the earth."

39

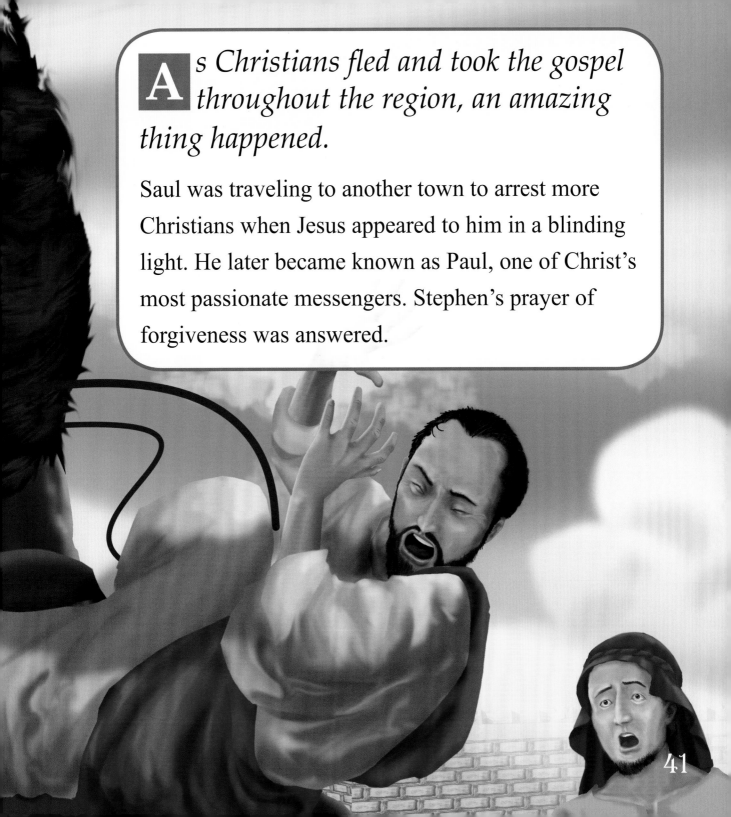

As Christians fled and took the gospel throughout the region, an amazing thing happened.

Saul was traveling to another town to arrest more Christians when Jesus appeared to him in a blinding light. He later became known as Paul, one of Christ's most passionate messengers. Stephen's prayer of forgiveness was answered.

41

Today, Christians are arrested and sometimes killed in countries around the world for telling others about Jesus.

In Pakistan, where most follow a religion called Islam, one young boy was courageous when he defended the Bible at school.

His teacher told him that the Bible had been changed. Standing among his classmates, he declared, "The Bible has not changed, but whoever reads it is changed."

Radical students yelled at him. But like Stephen, he stood firm.

Telling others about Jesus is not always easy.

We may not be arrested or hurt, but others may not like what we say and may want to find ways to keep us quiet. Just remember, we may be their only chance to hear about Jesus.

With the Holy Spirit's help, we can be courageous like Stephen and pray that Jesus will change their hearts.

For Reflection

"But in your hearts honor Christ the Lord as holy, always being prepared to make a defense to anyone who asks you for a reason for the hope that is in you; yet do it with gentleness and respect."
(1 Peter 3:15)

How did Stephen "give a defense" for (or show) the hope of Jesus in him?

What happened to Stephen when he defended the truth?

How did God help Stephen?

What does it mean to have "meekness and fear" when we stand up for Jesus? And how did Stephen show these qualities?

In what ways can we always be ready to tell others about Jesus?

Prayer

Dear Jesus,
Thank You for the peace and courage that You gave Stephen when he defended You. When someone asks me about You, help me to have that same courage so they, too, can experience Your hope. I pray for other Christians around the world who are hurt or imprisoned for telling others about You. Help them remain gentle yet bold.

Amen.

Bibliography

Kent, Homer A., Jr. *Jerusalem to Rome: Studies in the Book of Acts* (Grand Rapids, MI: Baker Book House, 1972).

Maddox, Robert L., Jr. *Layman's Bible Book Commentary* (Nashville, TN: Broadman Press, 1979).

Schaeffer, Edith. *Affliction* (Grand Rapids, MI: Raven's Ridge Books, 1993).

Willmington, Dr. H. L. *Willmington's Guide to the Bible* (Wheaton, IL: Tyndale House Publishers, Inc., 1984).

About The Voice of the Martyrs

The Voice of the Martyrs (VOM) is a nonprofit, interdenominational Christian missions organization dedicated to serving our persecuted Christian family worldwide through practical and spiritual assistance and leading other members of the body of Christ into fellowship with them. VOM was founded in 1967 by Pastor Richard Wurmbrand, who was imprisoned fourteen years in Communist Romania for his faith in Christ, and his wife, Sabina, who was imprisoned for three years. In 1965, Richard and his family were ransomed out of Romania and established a global network of missions dedicated to assisting persecuted Christians.

Be inspired by the courageous faith of our persecuted brothers and sisters in Christ and learn ways to serve them by subscribing to VOM's free monthly magazine. Visit us at persecution.com or call 1-800-747-0085. Explore VOM's five purposes and statement of faith at persecution.com/about.